brilliant water

Books by Christopher Merrill

Poetry
> *Workbook*
> *Fevers & Tides*
> *Watch Fire*

Nonfiction
> *The Grass of Another Country: A Journey Through the World of Soccer*
> *The Old Bridge: The Third Balkan War and the Age of the Refugee*
> *The Forest of Speaking Trees: An Essay on Poetry*
> *Your Final Pleasure: An Essay on Reading*
> *Only the Nails Remain: Scenes from the Balkan Wars*

As Editor
> *Outcroppings: John McPhee in the West*
> *The Forgotten Language: Contemporary Poets and Nature*
> *From the Faraway Nearby: Georgia O'Keeffe as Icon* (with Ellen Bradbury)
> *What Will Suffice: Contemporary American Poets on the Art of Poetry*
> (with Christopher Buckley)
> *The Four Questions of Melancholy:*
> *New and Selected Poems of Tomaž Šalamun*
> *The Way to the Salt Marsh: A John Hay Reader*

Translations
> *Anxious Moments*, prose poems by Aleš Debeljak (with the author)
> *The City and the Child*, poems by Aleš Debeljak (with the author)

brilliant water

poems by
christopher merrill

White Pine Press • Buffalo, New York

WHITE PINE PRESS
P.O. Box 236, Buffalo, New York 14201

Acknowledgments:

I am grateful to the editors of the following publications, in which some of these
poems first appeared: *Columbia: A Magazine of Poetry & Prose, Metre, New Orleans
Review, New Virginia Review, The Paris Review, Pequod, Pivot, Sahara, Salamander, Salt
Hill Journal, Seneca Review,* and *The Taos Review.*

"Daylillies: Instruction and an Elegy" and "The Bees" were published in *Poems for a
Small Planet,* edited by Robert Pack and Jay Parini. Hanover, NH: New England
University Press, 1995.

Publication of this book was made possible, in part, by public funds
from the New York State Council on the Arts, a state agency.

Book design: Elaine LaMattina

Printed and bound in the United States of America

Cover image: Paul Klee, "Little Port."
Copyright ©2001 Artists Rights Society (ARS),
New York/VG Bild-Kunst, Bonn.

Library of Congress Cataloging-in-Publication Data

Merrill, Christopher.
  Brilliant water : poems / by Christopher Merrill.
    p. cm.
  ISBN 1-893996-12-3   (pbk. : alk. paper)
    I. Title
  PS3563.E74517 B75 2001
  811'.54–dc21   2001017659

for Lisa, Hannah, and Abigail

It was a year of brilliant water.
—Thomas De Quincey

I

The Lake

We won't return. Like seeds, awkward as auks
With broken wings, we'll float across the lake
Below the monastery, avoiding snags,
And snakes, and swamped canoes wedged in the reeds.

Our reign is over. Say we stopped one day
Outside the water mill to search for grain,
To study the footprints of our enemies
—The Gauls and ghosts whose languages had tamed us.

Our horses bucked and whinnied: we were lost.
And when we looked up from the star charts and psalters
We had believed provided plots and orders
For the millennium, the horses were gone.

The trees, too. And the lake. The water was blue
Until it disappeared. The sluice gate opened
Onto nothing. The mill wheel rolled away.
Even our words dissolved: *The Gauls and ghosts...*

Only their tracks remained—and a forest of snags
From which snakes wriggled, and the snapping turtles
Sundered from shells and water fell like leaves,
And the canoes were clouds streaking a sky

Of drying mud and reeds... Why did we sign
Our languages and loves away? What star
Should we have followed? Who are these deaf-mutes
Guarding our catacombs, like birds of prey?

*

We won't return. Proud as the passenger
Pigeons enshrined in banks and the Museum
Of Desire, we'll dredge the lake for our lost crowns,
Scepters, and words which might have led us home.

Like poisoned pods—that's how we left our mark
On the wetlands the drying lake created,
The swamps and marshes in which nothing grew
As long as soap and ashes saved our souls.

Our reign is over. Say we stalked our ghosts
Up to the monastery, through the emptied
Landscape—save for the upright coffins that lined
The hills, like trees: we didn't cut them down.

There were loudspeakers blaring from the stairs
And stained glass windows: *Pray for the pilgrims laughing*
In the last chapter of the Book of Hoot.
Obey the revelations of the Rat.

The lions in the Colosseum: Nuns,
Remember them! What we remembered were
White horses lowering their heads to drink
Water on the verge of vanishing...

And then it all came back—horses, and trees,
And lake. Mist rose in sunlight, and we thought
It was the first day of Creation... No.
Our ghostly reign is over. We won't return.

*

Down from the monastery, in the empty
Fountain (to which a man and a woman came
One winter afternoon, on skis, and lunched
On bread and cheese, and drank a gold Chablis,

Then in the sun made love, two foundlings kissing
And groping for each other on cement
Cracked by the elements, singing and fondling
And following belly to breasts, and hips

To eyes and lips, while a loudspeaker squawked
Like a crow, and wine spilled over melting snow
And rumpled clothes, and under them the ice
In the cement thawed, like the frozen lake

Below, snow-covered, blinding in the sun,
Cracks widening along its banks), there is
A statue of a saint, stained by the bats
And pigeons roosting in the monastery,

One arm folded, the other broken off,
Its head and the inscription missing, leaves
Drifting around the base, a hat and gloves
Stuffed—with the wine bottle—into the drain.

—Now the loudspeaker cackles, warning the nuns
To stay in the courtyard on Judgment Day,
And the wind rises, and the lake turns white
With waves... Our reign is over. We won't return.

*

Charioteers, awake! The sun is rising,
Raking the moon and stars out of the sky,
And there are martyrs writhing at the gates
Of the Colosseum, praying for our souls.

A penitent will lead the horses past,
Black cats will scatter from the catacombs,
And women dressed in white will light the torches
Carried by slaves and senators alike.

Tinsmiths and tutors, captives and cavaliers
Who dream of water filling the arena,
Creating from the aqueduct a sea
In which mock naval battles can be fought—

All gather for the races and the plumes
Of dust the horses kick up, covering
The chariots; while the Barbarians
Assembling near the Forum dream of fire.

If the arena turns into a sea?
Water will wash off the earthen walls and floors
The blood of wild beasts sacrificed at dusk,
Sailors and saboteurs will steer their ships

Over the sunken pillars and labyrinths,
And a staged war will start, which will not end
Until the Empire falls... These are our ghosts
And Gauls, the ones who plotted out our reign.

*

Forget the opera canceled in Chianti:
The barren apple trees are holding sway.
And the mad orchardist is on the make,
Publishing the annals of his angst.

In March he used his neighbor's shears to prune
His trees, infecting them with a disease
No one could name; in May the blossoms turned
Grey; in June the limbs began to bleed.

And now in August he must count his losses
—Cash, apple sauce and cider, faith and women
He loved in Italy—then wait for autumn,
Season of miracles, and moneylending,

And opera—his passion, curse, and cure:
He loves the fat girl in the final act,
Whose voice can frighten boys into belief,
Or resurrect cabals and mystery cults.

Bravo! Bravo! he cried and clapped one night
In sleep, dreaming of horses, courtesans,
And evening promenades along the Arno.
And when he woke he sang, *We won't return...*

In autumn, he believes, the aluminum
Stepladders propped against his trees will draw
Lightning down from the skies, and the bare limbs
Will flare with fruit and music, women and wine.

*

An aging actor enters stage left, searches
The audience and prompter's box for his cue,
Then settles on a shadow in the wings
—The blonde assassin heading for the door.

The house lights flicker. The curtains freeze. A hush,
Like fog, spreads from the pit into the seats.
The actor, heeding the assassin's signals,
Slumps to the floor, begging her not to leave:

Remember our crusade against the past
And future—how we trained ourselves to speak
Only in tongues until we could discover
The names of all the infidels in Rome?

And how we smoked hashish behind the church,
Then snuck into the steeple to make love
While the choir rehearsed a requiem?
And how you rang the bell before you came?

Remember, please, the monastery fountain,
Where I proposed for us a life of pleasure
And prayer—and how (when you refused) I cried:
I want to be a hangman or a saint!

—And then she's gone... The curtains fall, and the crowd
Applauds. The actor bows, remembering
Her laughter in the steeple, and the bell,
And why she bleached her hair, vowing to leave him.

*

We won't return before the final act.
Say we're the prompters who can't find our place,
Turning the dog-eared pages of a script
We can't—or won't—decipher anymore.

And when the curtains rise we fall asleep.
The actor must look elsewhere for his cues.
He thinks the blondest usher is his wife
—Ex-wife, that is. She feeds him all his lines.

He calls her his assassin. Each night for her
He improvises on a theme, a scene
From their imaginary courtship, marriage,
Arguments, and divorce. She thinks he's crazy,

And hates the way he ends the show by chanting:
I want to be a hangman, not a saint!
She'd rather work for tips at the strip joint
Her father runs. Her mother won't allow it.

Applause for his performance, his bereavement,
Is what awakens us. The house lights shine.
The blondest usher's gone. *Give her a raise!*
The actor mutters as he leaves the stage:

Give everyone a raise, and bells to ring,
And a requiem to learn for Roman slaves
And saboteurs! Find me a rosary
And rope, black hood and habit: our reign is over.

*

Here in the Book of Hoot it says: *Beware*
Of pilgrims laughing at the lionized
Martyrs and gladiators still adrift
In the dust and waters of the Colosseum.

Guard against pundits trumpeting the end
Of opera and outings on the Seine,
Horse races, riots, and religious wars,
Auks, Gauls and ghosts, slick annals of desire.

And pray for all the nuns who disappeared
The night they watched a noblewoman slip
Into the lake below the monastery,
Loosening her long hair, shedding her clothes,

Her blouse and bonnet, skirt and underwear,
Which floated for a moment, like water lilies
About to close. She swam across the lake,
Climbed the steep bank by the abandoned mill,

And fell into the arms of the woodcutter
From the far north... Then they were gone. The nuns
Followed their footprints into the pure pages
Of a book unwritten in our dying language

Of love and loss... Coffins line the hills,
Not trees, and snakes are flying in formation.
The lake may empty in the dark, or freeze,
Or stay the same. But the nuns won't return.

*

Thus in the monastery garden herds
Of horsetail trample bleeding hearts and bloodroot,
The morning glories in the laurel hedge
Trumpet the end of the bad gardener's luck,

And foxglove blossoms shinny up their stalks,
The spikes at the top tearing open the veil
Of summer on the hill above the lake,
Revealing an old priest slumped in his chair.

A breviary's draped across his chest;
A pot of tea cools by his feet; the bell
Ringing behind him, ushering to prayer
Those he loved, will not awaken him.

Nor will he hear the loudspeaker announce
His elevation to the white beyond,
The world he once described in tracts and sermons
As the believer's holdings... His last thought?

An image of a couple making love
One winter afternoon, in the drained fountain,
Clothes and flesh flashing in the sun and snow,
Their cries in the clear air surprising him—

He never said a word about them, never
Believed what he had seen. Nor did he forget
The look of pleasure on the woman's face,
The man's excitement or his pain, the pain.

*

Now the mad orchardist is buttering
His hair, having already scorched the grass
Around his trees, burned his work shirt and boots,
And scuffled with a Frenchman at the fair.

He has no interest in his lineage
—The Gauls and ghosts who summon him at dusk
Down to the lake to watch a noblewoman
Parade around the water mill, calling

—In vain—for the woodcutter from Brazil
Or Nome, the hangman from the hinterland
Who taught her how to sing to the condemned
Men she would never pardon, or desert.

He uses butter only to betray
His coarser instincts—lust for aging whores,
Rage at his inability to flay
And gut a deer, dread of the known and numbered...

The Frenchman had blue eyes and a bad leg,
Rumors of war in Africa and guns
For sale. That's why the orchardist attacked him
Outside the big top, wrestled him to the ground,

Then gave him all his money and a map
Of the sky—and why he vowed to follow him
To the Red Sea... Now his hair is slick and full
Of flies. *We won't return*, he tells his ghosts.

*

The hooded man mounting the gallows stairs
Prays that the woman singing to him has
Pull with the hangman late for this appointment.
She sings without regard for fate or genius.

He listens to the wind rise off the lake
Behind him, thinking how a blind man uses
His other senses to "see," how afraid
He was the night his comrades killed that novice,

That traitor who had named names to the clerks
And priests determined to destroy belief
In possibility, in widening
Expanses of insight, in arabesques

Choreographed for the devout *and* damned...
–*Where is the hangman?* asks a deep voice. Then:
Are you prepared for ridicule, for your last
Rites? Who shall we send your ashes to?

He doesn't answer, doesn't slow his steps.
The woman is singing out of tune, and he
Would like to marry her, then flee. He wonders
Why he abandoned his guitar for war?

The rope around his neck will make him dance
Unless the hangman doesn't show. The woman
Sings nonsense now–a string of syllables
He "reads" in languages he doesn't know.

*

And these are the revelations of the Rat:
No one aboard this ship, this ark, will drown
Without receiving last rites, a gold watch
Set for the afterlife, and acting lessons,

Which you will need to play the roles deaf-mutes
Assign you in the catacombs. They know
How to decipher the inscriptions engraved
In your death masks—lines you must learn by heart.

On Judgment Day they'll show you how to move
The rocks guarding your remains, before the earth
Opens and empties all the graves and tombs
In which those saved by soap and ashes hide.

Perhaps you will escape this version of Hell—
Bats with bony faces squealing and swooping
Through caverns lined with glowing canisters
Of fuel spent to harvest your desire:

Fission, fenced archipelagoes surrounded
By rising seas, sequoias in sawmills,
And well-attended funerals, and sizzling
On bone-white dishes: smoking meats and sauces...

The deaf-mutes will direct you from a vault
You may not enter until your watches stop:
There you will learn when your reign ended, how high
The seas will rise, and why this ship is sinking.

*

The fair might never end, the saboteurs
Believed. So they cut holes in the circus tent,
Seeded the clouds, and blocked the entrances
To the exhibits torturers curated.

Rain poured on vendors, judges, and the judged,
On animals, and bored adults, and crosses.
Dirt turned to mud. A tractor sputtered, stalled.
No one drowned. And no one got away.

The ground became an ocean floor. Stuffed auks
Sailed out the door of the confessional.
Hail Mary! sang the saboteurs, anointing
The priests who stalked the crowd, like avatars.

Who are these Luddites? cried the torturers.
What legacy allowed them to return?
The water rose around the frightened crowd.
The saboteurs retreated to the hills.

Legacy? Sawyers trapped in poisoned mills,
And clouds the color of a failing bank,
And two ribbons for the irises
Grown in dried blood the torturers donated.

Nightfall: the holes in the big top were not stars.
The judges used crosses to navigate.
Animals bolted. Vendors treaded water.
The crowd might not remember anything.

*

The torturers were tired of emptying
The pockets of the saved, then adding up
The years they wouldn't spend in Hell or Heaven.
They wanted to return to Timbuktu.

How hard it was, night after night, to sharpen
Razors and answers for the clerks and priests
They never met! How much they missed their days
Of watching natives bathing in the Niger!

Torture had lost its luster for these men.
Bed of Procrustes, cattle prods, thumbscrews,
Pincer and tongs—these were the tools of the bored,
Not the devout. Water was good for drinking,

Not dripping over shackled heretics,
Who only longed to hurdle over crosses.
The torturers dreamed of escape, of women
Reciting poetry along the river,

The songs of the gunrunner from Charleville
—The one the clerks and priests warned them about:
Poet and pederast! Drinker of absinthe!
The torturers wished they had known him, too.

The women washing clothes in Timbuktu
Were singing to the sun before it set.
The torturers waited for the heretics,
Their razors stropped, their water buckets full.

*

The clouds would not come down. No senator
Refused to let his slaves attend the fire
Sale of the Empire. Concubines applauded
Those buying up the land around the Forum,

While vendors made a killing selling blue
Eyes and blond hair to the Barbarians
Awaiting orders to attack the rapt
And bloodied citizens in the Colosseum.

Will they rape everyone? our ghosts demanded.
Or will they save those lessons for the future?
What happened to the saboteurs from Gaul?
Why pillage the Museum of Desire?

Smoke on the Tiber. Only concubines
Could tally up the losses—poisoned seeds,
A script no one could read without a mirror
In which to translate a condemned man's prayers,

The naval battles postponed until the leaks
In the Colosseum were repaired, the names
Of all the infidels who fled from Rome
Before the Emperor woke from his slumber...

Martyrs and gladiators fell to their knees.
A lion locked in a cage roared. Stakes—signs
Dropped from the clouds. Torches burned. Pray for those
Who couldn't read or reign or ride away.

*

Displayed in the Museum of Desire,
Among the magazines and uncut films
Devoted to the genitalia
Of men and women glistening in oil,

And lingerie exhibits, and stuffed shrines
Of birds and beasts endangered or extinct
—These testimonies and tableaux vivants
Of unrequited love haunt visitors:

1. The orchardist wants the fat girl, the diva
Kneeling and singing until the curtains fall,
To be his wife, although she'll need four men
And prayer to get her on her feet again...

2. The aging actor wants his blonde assassin
To sign his will and witness his attempt
To speak in tongues to a deaf audience:
I have blue eyes for sale and slaves to free!

3. While the blondest usher wants to strip and slowly
Dance for the strangers who will make her mother
Jealous—and rich enough to move to Nome,
Leaving her all the nightly tips and offers...

4. The nuns and noblewoman want the man
Who tempted them to give up all they loved
—Mass and high tea, fox hunts and the way the sun
Blazed through stained glass windows, love notes, sign language...

*

Who are they anyway, the questioners
Who send us scripts to follow for each show
We put on for the lost and innocent?
Why don't they just go back to Timbuktu?

—That's what we found in the shipmaster's log
Before we sailed for Madagascar: *Bullwhips*
Mean nothing to us now! Our sentiments
Exactly—and we read no more that day!

But Madagascar, like Mount Sinai, sank,
According to the ancient stevedore,
The stowaway who wanted to return
To Rome. And still we hadn't saved our souls.

Doomed to repeat history—to perform mystery
Plays for the Gauls, not God, costumed in cowls
And cassocks, preaching miracles to sinners
Spared by the plague—we lined the deck, crying:

Is this the white beyond? Why does that wave
Look like the Wailing Wall? What made us sail
Around the world in search of golden calves?
Why have our watches stopped? Who are these mutes?

If only we had known that visionary
In Ankober, and drunk absinthe with him,
And spouted lines of verse at the night sky!
If only we had gone to Timbuktu!

*

These are the maps, star charts, and plot outlines
We never used, certain we knew the routes
To Sinai, Madagascar, and beyond.
Our reign is over. Judged. We won't return.

These are the pages—glued together, charred—
Of revelations no one may decipher
Before the floodgates open in the cities
The rich abandon to the innocent.

Here's water that will gush through theaters
And mausoleums, emptying the seats
Filled with men sleeping through the double feature,
And coffins moldering in walls, and the lake.

Here's brimstone that will burn through clouds, spilling
Ash over lovers riding horses past
The monastery fountain, believing nothing
Will change between them: *We won't drift apart!*

And here are the notes, like traps, set in tree stumps
Along the lake, summoning the last hangman,
The last woodcutter from Brazil or Nome,
To come down from the woods, don his black hood,

And go to work again. The gallows built
Behind the mill are lined with ghosts and Gauls,
Twelve heretics condemned in secret trials,
A noblewoman singing to herself.

II

The Fence

Once upon a time is what the fence dividing up a mountain range announces, in lines at once irregular and even.

For drama it depends upon a clear beginning, middle, and end. Its effects? Cathartic, purging landowners of their terror, interlopers of their pity. *On guard!* the playwright cries. *All the world's a fence,* the groundlings say.

In the ancient quarrel between fancy and the imagination the fence takes both sides. Nor does it distinguish between form and content, poetry and prose.

These are the four directions of the fence: up, down, right, wrong, black, white, male, female. Nevertheless at night the fence points only toward the future, time's true north.

In Tennessee someone is pouring the wilderness into a jar—that's one way to build a fence. Here's another: trace a pebble's lineage back to Creation.

Vested with moonflowers and intimations of the miraculous, the fence tilts into the hills, loosening its nails in a provocative fashion, unbuckling the armor men are saving for the final days.

See how the fence swaggers in the wind, embodying a dying sense of justice; how it casts a shadow over the rumpled sheets of mud tucked into an arroyo in the wake of a flash flood; how it reveals our weakness for design.

For we carried the fence, like our accents and dances, into the wilds of this sprawling continent, where it survived our twangs and replaced our two-steps.

This is where we sang until our throats—our thoughts—were raw. And this is what results from myth giving way to law and history. Who will accept the fence's first, and final, offer?

The earth itself is a fence, according to the cartographers of the afterlife, in a universe awash in fences—a belief the demographers reject. Obscured by the rivers and rock walls the fence crosses and climbs is one stark fact: whether the world ends in fire or ice, the fence will live happily ever after.

Reckonings

for Patrick de Freitas

God, *what a feeling!* we declared
At the surfing championship, convinced the election
Had been rigged. We knew the minister of culture
Would never make it to the finals, never
Address the caterers setting up the tent. The dune
Buggy races would be postponed. And no one could explain
Why the beach was littered with spare parts
For the Air Force. Everyone had a story, especially the women
From Gibraltar, of encountering grizzly bears and families
Pocked by incest... Meantime the canyons were burning.
Couples lay on their roofs to watch the progress
Of the fire leaping from ridge to ridge,
Igniting whole stands of timber. Yes, it *was* a feeling
Vague as the spray the surfers kicked up with their boards.
Pilots and generals were hiding in the wings
Of theaters across the country, waiting
For the smoke to lift. The election results
Might be announced at any moment. And the waves?
The waves were bigger now: one carried a contestant
Miles down the beach, then left him churning in the water.

Day Lilies: Instructions and an Elegy

for Robert Jebb (1944-1990)

Plant them with shadows in mind, under a dying
Cottonwood, in a bed of bone meal and arrowheads.
Lather the soil with humus or Apache tears
—The drops of sleek obsidian culled from the creek
Below the slumbering volcano. Use the tools
—A spading fork, a trough—of the illiterate
Day laborer who studies numerology
And cannot count; like him, you must work in the dark.
Thus wake and bathe before sunrise on the Day of the Dead.
Gather supplies—a burlap sack, a bone-shaped loaf
Of bread, death's-heads to hang from every door. Then wait.
At nightfall dig the flowers from a roadside ditch.
Hum no dirges while you divide the clumps; only
Waltzes will do. Pray for the pilgrims killed last Easter
Marching to a church built on sacred ground: the blessed
Dirt that lured them to that shrine, that might have healed
Their relatives' infirmities—a limp, or fading
Vision, or infertility—may save your transplants
From the flash floods and droughts that score and scorch this canyon.
Cover the roots with charms against mule deer and dogs.
Then count, O count next June the short-lived blooms—the yellow
Swans preening in the sun, then disappearing at dusk;
The blaring lemon trumpets no one listens to;
The orange bells that ring now for the hummingbird
And not for you, my friend, who might have planted them.

Lines on the Winter Solstice

A day of creaks and croaking! Ice in the skylight,
Three ravens in the apple tree the migrants missed,
Lengths of seasoned aspen crackling in the stove
—So much has changed. The irises were never planted,
And squirrels ate the poppy seeds saved for the border.
Mice feed on the wires; rows of onions buckle under
Another foot of snow; next spring, the frozen garden
Hoses, unwound, will crack... A raven flaps away,
The branches shake, and a half-eaten apple plops
Into the kindling pile: if only you were here.

The Bees

After a bear ransacked their hive, strewing wood, wax,
And honey over grass, and rabbit brush, and asters,
Trampling worm-eaten apples and a peach tree bending
Into the earth, arming the orchardist who loathed
Nocturnal creatures more than an early snow—the bees
Tunneled through twigs and leaves, stones and tar, burrowing
Into the roof and ceiling of a house—an estate
The absent owners wouldn't visit, settle, or seize.

Around the queen they wintered in the insulation.
And on the first warm day of spring they fell from the rafters
Into the living room, a snowpack severing
Its hold on a hillside, then flooded over walls
Of photographs, last year's phone book, throw rugs and shag,
Buzzing the dusty windows and a dying jasmine,
To cluster on the sun-raked sill, prepared to gather
Pollen and nectar from the flowers still outside.

When snowmelt swelled the creek and irrigation ditch,
And the trees whitened, like a ring of moons revolving
Around the orchard, and the bear stirred in its den
High on the mesa overlooking the estate,
The orchardist loaded his gun and hid at dusk
Among his falling blossoms, the squall of lights the owners
Had never seen. Inside, the phone rang. Stopped. Lamps glowed.
The bees swarmed the locked doors, fireplace screen, floor. The house
       hummed.

Three Weeds

Horsetail

Swishing the flat backs of boxwood and stone,
The stems of dusty miller, and a spread
Of daffodil leaves drying in the sun,
The horsetail rears, unbridled, wild as seed.

It gallops through the garden, leaving its shoots
And markings everywhere. It drags the hired man,
Who twisted a rope of roots around his wrists
And waist, down to his knees. And when the twine

Breaks, the rushes bolt, trampling flower
Borders and beds, strewing their litter through
The compost pile, until one stalk, one augur
Of empire, clears the wall and lopes away.

Purple Loosestrife

Another interloper staking out its claim—
These spires of purple loosestrife moving through the ranks
Of roadside swamps and ditches, these slick managers
Of a vast seed system, of bees and wind and water,
Weed out reeds and rushes with the diligence
Of an auditor denying ordinary deductions.
Yet here it is dissolving differences again:
To calm a team of oxen driven mad by mosquitoes,
The plowman cuts a switch of willow-herb and whips
The backs of the broad animals, clearing the air.

Fireweed

For towhees, mice, and mule deer, fireweed blazes
A trail into the underbrush, a violet

Smoldering overtaking ruts the road
Crew, like a flash flood, left—a path no one

Will follow home tonight... This is the fire
An orphan fans, hitchhiking toward the pass,

Cursing the ones who walked away from him.
The fever raging in the rear-view mirror

Of a woman in a pickup, pulling over
To let him in. The burning. The flowering.

Mercy

At twilight the horse thief torches the cross
Propped in the river, ashes cover the bank
Like a beard, and the bridge disappears in smoke.

The driver of the jackknifed milk truck sleeps.
The swimmers on the white road shave their bodies,
Afraid to dive into the burning water.

Three cars skid off the road and stall in pools
Of milk. The faithful on the bank have barbells,
A sense of charity, piano music,

And poodles that need neutering. No one
Has a white horse. And no one cares. The thief
Hides in the woods, burying his crop and saddle.

The bridge is either open or missing, black
Or white. The swimmers gliding underwater
Avoid the drowning penitents and pearls.

There is no music here, no other way
Across the river. The dogs howl at the truck.
In the moonlight the road begins to glow.

Dog Days in Vermont

The cistern on the hill, sucked dry and sizzling
In the midmorning sun, cracks like a gourd.
Sticks and stones fill the pipes, and the pump rattles
Its bones—a sick man heaving in his bed.

Out of the kitchen faucet rust and water
Trickle toward the drain. Stop. A stack of plates,
Crusted together on the counter, seasons
Our squabbling over who will call for help.

This is an evil time. The heat returns,
Like an allergy. Asthmatics and assassins,
Escaping from the smoking cities, meet
In the Catskills, at weddings on the Cape.

And wild dogs from the trailer up the road
Are running mad around this mountain village,
Eluding bounty hunters and the police,
Attacking loggers, livestock, newlyweds.

The woman I will marry is afraid
To leave our rented farmhouse; afraid to stay,
I haul buckets of water from the spring.
I keep the owner's rifle by the bed.

High noon: the weed-choked pond seethes in the sun.
A hollow tree rocks back and forth, sagging
Into the water and creaking like a porch.

Mosquitoes, bullfrogs, crows—a cluster of nouns
Ripening on the vine of a single phrase—
Listen and wait. Cattails sway in the heavy air.

Call this the grammar of decay: the slough
Oozing around itself, collecting light
And larvae and dried moss curling into commas.

What can we learn here of the afterlife?
That it breeds pestilence, like an investment
Banker who cheats his clients and his firm?

How hard it is to read the sun-bleached signs
Our neighbor's nailed to rotting posts and hung
From the barbed wire protecting his domain.

The peeling paper sheds his threats: NO HUNTING,
FISHING, TRESPASSING HERE! NO LOITERING!
ALL VIOLATORS WILL BE... shot, I guess.

Along one bank irises hide a sleeping
Water snake. Clumps of reeds, which ring the sludge
And slurry, crackle in the heat, like kindling.

Say the pond's on fire—a wild baptismal
Fire, which in other ages burned us clean—
A font in which our vision and belief

Might clear: if only I could purify
The speech of my own tribe, my clan of doctors
And widows, mutterers and righteous men,

Dipping the language in this burning pool.
Ah, to speak in tongues, to preach the truth
Of prophets and fanatics... No, no, no.

This pond is where our neighbor's cattle drink,
The herd of Holsteins lumbering through the trees,
Swishing their tails, like scourges, at the brambles,

Nervous (perhaps) about the packs of dogs
That roam the hills beyond the pasture, howling
Into the night: a stock pond, not a symbol.

A water strider glides across the surface,
Tightening underwing the scum's green skin,
Like a percussionist tuning a drum.

And when the swamp grass flares, and the frogs croak,
And a crow stains the air, its harsh notes hanging
Like sumac berries from the sky, the snake

Wakens and, slithering into the deep,
Drags with it all my terror, all my pride.
If only I could learn to love you well.

———————

Weeding the landlord's kitchen garden: here are
Strawberries sprawling in spent and tangled vines,
Potato hills ribboned with bald tires, rows
Of bolting lettuce—seeds the wind will scatter
In the tall grass and goldenrod of what
Was pasture once. A woodchuck's watching us—
Two figures bent and shimmering in the heat,
Hoeing the sun-scorched earth through which it burrows.

Sweat marks and sweat, no-see-ums and mosquitoes,
A broken shovel. What's missing in this picture?
How we inherited our first days here
The harvesting of strawberries for breakfast,
And frozen daiquiris, and glacé pies;
How it was dark enough each night in bed
To mistake eyes for lips; how innocent
We were about the howling in the distance...

Corn withering on its stalks, in browning husks
That scrape the air. Something's eating the beans.
Storm clouds rise in the mountains rinsed with acid
Rain, where there must be a swimmer bracing
Herself for burning water, and a logger
Examining ridges of dying trees.

Behind us, like an ax, the phone rings, splitting
The house in half—into the past, the future.

———————

The leeches in the spring,
Our nettled swimming hole
Lined with a bath tub
Lifted from the village dump,

Cling to our backs and legs
When we emerge from the water,
Refreshed—if not released
From work and argument.

To draw them out, we huddle
Around the kitchen table,
Light matches by their bloated
Bodies, and pull, leaving

Across *our* bodies maps
Of blotches we may follow
Into the dark. Nothing
Will break this fever now.

———————

Up the unlit stairs we climb at dusk,
Asking: Will the heat lightning turn to rain
And fill the cistern? Will we sleep... or fight?

Undressing in the dark, then stuffing pillows
Under the door—to no avail. All night,
From room to room, mosquitoes track our spoor.

Bloodstained sheets, sweating mattresses, words, holes
In every screen: the owner's manual
On love says nothing about sleepless nights.

The oak beams in the ceiling spin. A lamp
Falls to the hardwood floor... and doesn't break.
Two faucets whine until I shut them off.

A pickup roars around the bend, a pebble
Ticking in one hubcap, like a second hand.
A shotgun blast. Then silence. Then a moan...

Then daybreak, when we rise, exhausted, to walk
Our neighbor's hills and fields, where horses sleep
Like statues and corn hunches in the wind.

The stars in our fenced heavens—how they strain
Imagination's limits, how they fade...
Even the dogs are sleeping in their pens.

Rosehips

for Marvin Bell

This false fruit, tear-shaped and smooth as a glass eye, cracks like pottery fired too quickly in a kiln. It reddens as it ripens, a line of yellow blearing. It's the smallest bird cage: inside, surrounded by an ocher sponge on the verge of rotting, are seeds and wings that soaked up sunlight in the thistles; freed, they flutter among the lodgepole pines at the pasture's edge, they float into the grass trampled by the horses that vanished in the night. Five leaves sprout from the pod, like the eyebrows of a woman who will travel constantly, in a small community. Rainwater on the leaves, and on the exposed roots of a dying aspen—a squirrel that skimmed across the pasture, like a stone. If you try to uproot the rose, you will shred your hands—the sharp thorns are thickest on the greying stems and branches near the base; only the green wood at the top is safe for stroking, though even here an emerging thorn may hook your finger.

What can you catch now that the horses are gone? The way they bolted through the open gate, followed a trail into the woods, and galloped up a canyon no one has ever explored... Or else the water trough coated with pine needles, two feed bins steeped in falling leaves, a rusted chain girdling the aspen, a fence built by the woman who cares for injured raptors and burrowing owls, a glimpse of circus animals in a caravan of clouds encircled by a rainbow, clumps of a wildflower about to burst out of its buskins to cure the vision of a myopic child—the boy who rolls these pods, like marbles, across the ground, and watches the squirrel watching him.

Door

for Olivia Gilliam (1938-1993)

How the sun lights the fuses of the sky-
Rockets arranged around this alpine meadow—
A battery of charges set and timed
And steaming in the noonday heat, bright streamers
And airbursts landing on dry slopes then down
These drainages: a world of flare and fade—
Scarlet explosions muffled in a swirl
Of sage and lupines, the spent cartridges
Scattered among divisions of pine seedlings,
Reserves of purple asters, and a team
Of mules-ears rounded up by wind and rain,
All aiming at the mountains, moose, and deer,
At hummingbirds, nocturnal moths, and the marsh,
Where the sandhill crane calls and calls, her song
The sound of someone opening a door...

Grammar

A garter snake's head pressed to the pavement—
And yet the taper of its body burns:

A sentence fragment for an earnest beetle
Rippling the snake's slick skin, like wind on water,

Conjugating fall—how milkweed spills
Into the air blown mustard seeds will season,

While a child flattens oak leaves in a book,
A woman stretches a black elastic band

Around a letter destined for the fire,
And in the tar a striped snake warms itself.

Inflections

for Lisa

The aging matriarch lost, in a stroke, her verbs,
As when a lightning bolt scorches and splits a white oak,
And the leaves close, like fists, and yet hang on until fall.
She's all nouns and no action now—*My husband gone.*
Church? Time? What day? Cold. Everything's implied, entwined
(As politicians know) in her inflections, in the way
Her pitch and cadences lure meaning from a word.

In spring and fall, when clouds swell above this bellied lake,
A string of crestless waves crashes against the mountains
And washes back into this remnant of a sea
Whose epic scope over the eon has diminished
To lyric status—a soiled pocket filled with salt,
A world in which nothing lives save brine shrimp and flies:
Enough to make and unmake our weather maps and patterns.

That chokecherry wallowing in the watercress,
Its trunk sliced open like an eye, hundreds of candles
Lighting the blossoms up and down the avenue
Of its limbs and branches—caught by a late snow, it drifts
Among the crucifers a Chinese family picks,
In the green procession stalled beside their salad bucket,
In the herbs Romans used to salve a bitten mind.

The rule about the rainbows at the matriarch's—
Catch and release, her gardener warned—we just ignored,
Fishing that pair of algae-covered ponds, those eyes
With cataracts, drawing our barbed hooks through the film
Until it flared. *Our* eyes were bigger in those days,
And like the trout that struck at leaves, twigs, scum, and shadows
Of swallows, we believed we would escape untouched.

Once, dead-drunk, face down in a pool of leaves, I watched
A salamander frozen to a mountain road
Take fire, lift its stiff limbs, and burn a hole in the air.

Thus the word moves some mornings until it's warm enough
To skitter back into the underbrush, the nouns
And adjectives lining the roads I cut in the page,
The verbs that first invade my disturbed areas.

———————

In daybreak's sift and swirl I found butter-and-eggs
Swelling in a scrubbed pan, in the ash and gravel basin
Sloping down from the road; a haul of shivered logs;
Pine cones hooked by the gills and hanging from the lines
Squirrels set out last night; the wind's ripples and falls;
Dried scales of sunlight flaking on the river bank;
A rooster crowing in the woods, waking no one...

———————

I wanted to tell you that the ivy scraping the window
Etched in a message beyond recall; that the wind
Ushering in the guests, the floodwaters rushing through
The houses of the men who cleared these hills, might lead us
Back from temptation; that when I saw you at the door,
Listening to the warbler, I thought of the pilot who breaks
Through fog to find himself over the runway—and dives.

Sagebrush

for Aleš Debeljak

These are the last days of its empire. No flags fly from its dead limbs, nor do its branches lost to age or blight bend in the wind. Only two outposts remain, two settlements of grey and green, in the largest house of which the general lifts his fork before casually signing marching orders for his starving troops. Here in a field of shrunken cabbages the asthmatic priest wakes in the night, gasping. Foot soldiers reach for their inhalers. Courtesans bronze their nails. In a world of whiskers and spent flowers there are always rumors of barbarians gathering beyond the barbed wire the prisoners strung across the last meadow on our maps. Even our bravest cartographer prefers the company of the general to wandering past that fence, though the general will never share his food. No doubt a messenger from the capital is already on his way to the first outpost, bearing orders for our retreat. Who will inherit the promise of these stiff limbs? Ants, grass, and wind. What is the price of wisdom here? Only the priest and prisoners can tell.

Sestina on Six Words by Vicente Huidobro

An angel rises from the new volcano.
Clocks and steam engines spill into the sea.
This is how the scholar builds his city.
And this is how to fake a suicide:
At nightfall trap and fricassee a dove,
Then feed it to the sailors who cannot sleep.

The scholar never needs to eat or sleep,
Or so believes the new guide to the volcano,
Who also thinks sailors can follow a dove
From island to island, across the sea,
And not end up committing suicide.
He left his watch and compass in the city.

Tear down the ramparts of the mythic city!
The guide cries. *It's too quiet there to sleep.*
The angel savors words like *suicide*
And *faith.* The scholar wants to scale the volcano
Before its lava cools into a black sea
Nothing will feed in save the unfledged dove.

He can remember how the angel dove
Into the moat around his books, his city,
Shrieking, *It's time to starve the fevered sea!*
He wonders why he can no longer sleep—
And why the guide ditched him at the volcano.
He plans to write a tract on suicide.

The angel? She wants every suicide
To be absolved by the song of the mourning dove
Circling the swelling cone of the volcano.
The mariners marooned outside the city
Must drain the moat before they sail or sleep.
The scholar counts the clocks ticking in the sea.

Steam rises like an angel from the sea.
The sailors stop another suicide.
The guide believes he can lull lava to sleep,
Though not without the cooing of the dove
The scholar dreamed of in the holy city.
Faith, like an island, grows from a volcano.

What sea or fiction begat suicide?
Who sailed to the volcano with the dove?
Guide, angel, scholar, city—no one can sleep.

Jaime Sabines:
From *Something on the Death of the Elder Sabines (Part One)*

X

It's a long bad dream,
a stupid horror movie,
an endless tunnel
full of rocks and puddles.
What a wicked time this is,
spinning the hours and years,
dream and conscience,
the open eye and slow death!

XI

Newborn in the bed of death,
a peaceful creature, still, soft,
an infant of the sun, dark-faced,
swaddled in the crib of silence,
nursing on darkness, empty-mouthed,
extinguished eyes, deserted heart.
Plugged lung, my child, old man,
buried heaven and spring of the air,
I'm going underground, a deep sob,
so I can see you once again.

XIV

The glass you drank from hasn't broken,
nor the bowl, the lamp, the plate.
The bed you died in hasn't burned,
we didn't sacrifice a cat.

You outlived everything. Everything exists
despite your death and my despair.
Maybe life attacks us
the way cancer burned through your shoulder.

We buried you, wept for you, died for you,
you're really dead, fucked over, sterile,
while we think of what we didn't do

and want you back—even if you're ill.
Nothing you were, we were, us and you,
is like what's living in your hell.

XVI
(November 27)

Can you open your eyes and see us now?
Can you hear us?
Hold your hands out for a moment?

We're by your side. This is our party,
old man, your birthday.
Your wife and children, nieces and nephews,
we've all come to hold you, old man.
Listen!
Don't go and cry like us
—your death is our excuse
to cry for the world,
for the living.
There's a fallen wall between us,
only the body of God, only His body.

Ash Wednesday

A wire sparks in the live oak, scorching limbs
And leaves, igniting tufts of Spanish moss:

A hiss and sizzle overhead, a burning
In the spring air, smoke coiled then slithering
Along the street down to the dying river—

That's where the workers up since midnight gather
Masks, beads, and litter from the last parade.

The penitents march off to church. A gardener
Spreads ashes over flower beds. I wait
To hear the turning latch, your voice at the door.

New Orleans

The Garden

A thread of sun-bleached hair spun into the iron
Grillwork surrounding the balcony: morning
Glory, which rings its white bells at nightfall,
Calling to order insects, birds, and cats.
Weeds in a whiskey barrel planter sink
Their teeth into the tar paper floor, demanding
To be pulled. The potted coleus, a mulched
Core of blood-colored sheaths, gives way to the wind,
The maidenhair fern lifts its feathery slip,
And ashes in oyster shells begin to swirl.
Here comes the tree of heaven's golden rain.
And here you come: hail, lightning, and desire.

———————

Blonde, barefoot, and married to my friend—
And while she works in their bedroom, correcting
Galleys for a new encyclopedia
Of modern thought, I sit at the electric
Company's abandoned spool, the desk
Her husband uses now, and watch two boys
Bicycling in the alley down below.
Theirs is a circle of screams tightening
Around a patch of concrete the sun will never reach,
A set of bound roots that girdles a tree—
Fucker! one screams. The word rises like a weed.
Fuck! cries the other. Windows rattle shut.

———————

If I could reclaim that light or language,
The promise of our summer in the garden,
Our season of strawberries and milk snakes;
If I tapped the night's supply of ink
And traced the same hieroglyphs in our sheets,
Recovering the drift of that warm wind;
And if I found a way to write again
That poem praising the day you drew your bow
Over the strings of the last elm, tuning
The leaves to the pitch of your cry before they fell;—

Would you forgive the ravages of storm
And blight, our dwindling harvests, the snow's blank staves?

Should, Should Not

variation on a theme by Czeslaw Milosz

I should have pocketed the key left in the front door of the embassy and used it to discover the fate of the Lost Tribes, sneaking in one night to read the minutes from their last meeting.

I should have worn gloves to the Inauguration Ball, where I was criticized for my attire—my hair shirt and sandals, helmet and scabbard.

I should not have kissed the famous chef on both cheeks, praising him for the delicacy with which he fricasseed the entrails of my enemies, nor should I have ordered my father to dump the punch bowl over the archbishop's head, prompting a mass conversion among movie stars and the media.

I should have insisted that the minister of sport amnesty the deserters fleeing to Istanbul, instead of allowing him to behead the soldiers who had boarded up the windows of my favorite brothel.

I should not have copied the cuckoo's example, refusing to build my own house, tricking others into raising my offspring. Likewise I should not have forged the names of the dead at Waterloo in order to inherit their political beliefs and taste for carnage.

I should have called for an inquest into my behavior at the polo match, where a large swastika was burned into the grass near my opponents' goal and no one claimed responsibility for the mysterious deaths of all the horses.

I should not have eavesdropped on the ex-president reciting old speeches to himself in the middle of the night; nor believed that anyone except his wife and bodyguards would heed his renewed calls for aerial bombardment of active volcanoes; nor imagined that his declaration of a permanent state of emergency in the relations between men and women was false.

I should have tuned the choir of orphans condemned to sing for their meals before turning them loose in the streets, removed from their reading lists all revolutionary tracts, and offered them instructions in etiquette.

I should not have sunk the garbage scow patrolling the Atlantic seaboard, nor saved the bandages and needles that washed up along the beach, nor exiled the hemophiliacs afraid of the sun and the sight of blood.

I should have sent out a press release detailing the fortunetelling feats of the Gypsies arriving from Transylvania to monitor our elections, then boiled the drinking water drawn from the Lethe before serving it to the heads of state celebrating the impending triumph of democracy.

I should not have tempted the missionaries along the Amazon to learn so many native languages instead of mastering their sailing skills, nor should I have let their superiors cut down every tree in the rain forest in lieu of passing on the hunting lore entrusted to them by their first hosts—the one-breasted women armed with bows and arrows.

I should have crossed my heart when we tried to patch the hole in the sky, shoveled salt over my shoulder at the sight of the fireball plummeting into the sea, made a wish before the solar wind blew out all the lights.

I should have checked the ferry schedule for the river Styx.

I should have asked Charon for permission to troll.

I should have thrown back what I caught.

III

Where the Smoke Comes From

Mangoes in Moscow—and a biplane circling
Red Square, dropping leaflets and invitations
To the masked ball Count Tolstoy throws each year
To celebrate the anniversary
Of his death: a blizzard of white paper falling
Over church domes and kiosks, saboteurs
And spies sent by a minister in Minsk,
Into the hands of the goose-stepping guards,
The opera singer with a burning throat,
The one-eyed coachman waking from a binge.

Only the woodcutters from the count's estate
Will miss his annual affair: they're afraid
Of the women he imported from the Tropics,
Who traded their grass skirts for battle-axes,
The ones who hide among the arsonists
Plotting to raze the palace and the church
In which the czar's elite, the soldiers bred
For bravery and ballroom dancing, vowed
To keep journals recording all their conquests—
Religions, languages, and noblewomen...

The count will read selections from his journals
At midnight, in the den, to anyone
Dressed in a peasant's shift who promises
To marry him. His handwriting's precise,
The entries dated, numbered, and described
From every angle. Coded. Starred. The subject?
A young man stalking himself in the mirror
Of women... *Now the unmasking must begin
For moneylenders and adulterers,*
The count will say. And it will start with him.

———

Baked mangoes served with Brie and suckling pig
A Cossack smuggled in from Istanbul
—A journey costing him his innocence,
Commission, mistresses, white horse, and hair:

That's why he hoards the shrapnel in his knee
And waves his pistol at the silverware.

The wine? A Burgundy from the Black Sea,
Selected by the Sultan of Brunei
And aged in the oak hold of a slave ship
A band of penitents seized in Suez,
Sailed like an old man to Byzantium,
And moored one Easter near a monastery.

Dessert will be a reading from our psalter:
Charity begins at war, not home,
Among the Ottomans attacking Greece
Only to let a troop of Cretans go,
Because their humor's equal to their faith
In alphabets and olive groves... Cream? Sugar?

Resist not evil, the chef commands his crew,
The spirit fighters scouring the kitchen floor
With fire and brimstone from the final act
Unfolding in the Book of Hours: *Imagine*
Typhus and lions rampant in a prison
—They will be the heralds of your new world order!

No one shall leave the ball without a guide
To vegetarian cuisine and care
For prisoners of war. A burning glass
May clarify the count's dream: that the fire
He calls belief, the flaming field of prayer
Engulfing his starved guests, may save us all.

———————

The catacombs (in which the alchemist's
Daughter is weighing out fool's gold and silver
Saved for the afterlife) will open soon,
According to the pistol-waving Cossack.

He learned this in a dream in Tuscany
Before he had to flee his creditors,
Before he lost his favorite horse and hair,
His mistresses and memory. What else?

He dreamed of sailing to Byzantium
With his inheritance, a first edition
Of *The Illuminations*, and a plan
For raising saints and tyrants from the dead.

He dreamed of questioning a prisoner
In Babylonian and writing down
The answers in cuneiform—to be deciphered
By scholars, not a military judge.

Then he dreamed about the bomb in the bazaar:
The flare and flashing, shrapnel tearing up
Silks, sizzling meats, and his own skin, the smell
Of ether in a tent, a gleaming saw...

He wishes now he could remember why
He once believed in alchemy, in grace.
The dark-haired woman from his dream? *A harlot
Or a heretic*, he might have told himself

Before he woke in Istanbul, bloodied
And bartering with an Etruscan merchant
Escaped from history—the catacombs,
That is, in which a woman anyone

Could love was mixing chemicals, waiting
For an elixir to emerge from the notes
Her father had assembled in his cell
And bribed a drunken guard to smuggle out—

Notes on the art of transformation: age
And iron into gold, speech into song,
Men who could live *without the spirit of God*,
Charts for the seas and channels of desire...

Deep in the earth, unable to make out
The code and meaning of these notes, the woman
Summoned the Cossack in a suite of dreams,
Offering him fictions and prophesies.

What will she show him in the catacombs?
The diaries of czars and anchorites,
Despots and hermits fasting in the desert,
Illiterates and angels from Ardennes...

What shall he call her, then? *Anna Karenina*,
The count will tell him. *Catherine the Great*,
His army friends might say. And in the snow
The one-eyed coachman mumbles, *Isis, Isis.*

In the count's dream his *Resurrection* was
Under review. A critic who had scorned
His stories and marriage, pamphlets and conversion,
Was holding forth on water quality:
Soon all the oceans, all the streams will turn
To salt. And nomads armed with vipers, stones,
And maps to the oasis will refuse
To dance for rain. And statues of Poseidon
Will march us up the hill in Calvary,
Where in our goblets we'll find blood, not wine...

The critic waltzed across his study, smoking,
Surrounded by bookshelves sprawled on their sides.
I have Count Tolstoy's new work on my shelf,
He muttered, waving his cigar at the books
Cluttering the floor. Then he recited the titles—
Nookie at Noon, If You Can't Live Without Me

Why Aren't You Dead?, and *But Enough About You*—
On either side of Tolstoy's last great novel.
And that was all... Or so the dreamer thought
Until he woke in his tub, shivering,

A samovar at one end and a snake
Slithering down the drain. A train was leaving
The station in Siberia or Rome,
And he would never find another ticket
To the afterlife, not while the tub was filling
With salt. Smoke rose around him. The prostitute?
Say the count fell in love with his creation.
And say he will return as a streetwalker
From St. Petersburg—if not a cockatoo,
A palomino, or a Wandering Jew.

————————

The opera singer has a new white horse,
Consumption, and a crush on the one-eyed
Coachman: no cockatoo or Wandering Jew.

No music either for her last recital.
Only a tuning fork with which to strike
The coachman's knee: his reflexes are slow—

And in the drunken key of C. Her mare
Would canter through Red Square, if she could wrest
Its reins and bit out of her coachman's mouth.

She tests her voice. He whinnies in his sleep.
Her blood-stained handkerchiefs clutter the house.
His monocle is a mirror for the future.

And the sky is full of letters no one answers.
Yet who can read the map to the oasis
Without believing in the afterlife?

Take. Eat. This is the salt of my forgiveness,
The body of the zealot I once was,
The singer whispered when the dam was opened,

Flooding Siberia and Rome, Egypt
And Istanbul—the dam the prophets built
And passed down through the scribes of Babylon

To carpenters and choreographers,
Sopranos, seamstresses, and the elite
Soldiers who gathered in the palace courtyard

To taunt the czar... The water turned to ink,
And in the Black Sea slaves and slavers scribbled
Instructions for the saboteurs from Minsk;

Devotions for the coachman hurrying
From mistresses to ministers and back;
And for the dying singer? A libretto,

For which her pianist refused to write
Music she could perform without rehearsing—
And without bloodying the stage and pit...

Thus her recital will consist of silent
Prayers for consumptives and a requiem
For voice, fire, bridle, count, and Wandering Jew.

But she needs footlights, listeners, and time.
Perhaps a cockatoo to wake the guard
Outside the concert hall. The Wandering Jew?

She and the count think he's in Calvary,
Hiding among the thieves. Her palomino
Neighs in the stable, and her maid's confused:

Who built that dam—and why? Where were the scribes
After the water turned to salt and sand?
What aria will you perform? No answer.

Enter stage left: *Into the mouth of the wolf,*
The coachman mumbles, dusting his monocle.
Let the wolf die, the singer coughs and cries.

————————

An agate in a sack of yellow onions:
That's what a revolutionary is,

According to the Cossack waving his gun
At the woodcutters picketing the ball.

He eyes the samovar, and silverware,
And soldiers lining up against the wall,

Imagining the next utopia:
Serfs with good teeth, maids dumping chamber pots

On civil servants, parades of shackled priests,
Vodka distilled from black potatoes, war

Between the rich and the recalcitrant,
The Ural Mountains and twelve angry miners...

Yet if he still believed in alchemy
Or could return to Rome and Istanbul,

He might imagine maids in judges' robes,
Wine from the Black Sea, speeches ripening

Like mangoes on the tongues of spirit fighters,
Trains stalling halfway to the afterlife.

The catacombs! The catacombs! he cries.
That's where I lost my mistresses and hair!

(His horse? He gave her to the opera singer,
Who promised to canter around Red Square,

Where the white mare bucks at the sight of soldiers
Blindfolded, shaking, waiting for their final

Orders to be delivered in the form
Of a firing squad. And when the triggers click

The horse neighs—neighs and bolts and gallops away.
The Cossack winces. The woodcutters freeze...)

And it was in Byzantium that I found
Anna Karenina hiding from the count,

Hustling merchants in the bazaar. Isis,
I exclaimed, save our country from outsiders!

And she replied, Only desire may spare
Your century from itself—but who will be

Your prophet of the body? Who will write
Prayers for the naked and the saved? Or pray?

Then she was gone—into the silks and sauces,
Where a bomb exploded... and I lost my way.

The Cossack aims his pistol at the woodcutters,
Samovars, soldiers, firing squad, and sky,

Then shoots a window out and spreads his coat
Over the hole, whispering, *Rest in peace...*

The diva, meanwhile, wants to sleep with him,
Or sing an aria in Syrian,

Or use these glass slivers to shred the dress
She sewed herself for her farewell recital.

Over the heads of the picketers she drapes
Her bloodied handkerchiefs: *I'm the mad hatter*

Of Madagascar, she explains, *a role*
Only consumptives may audition for.

If you want to join my entourage,
Become my coaches, make-up artists, and prompters,

You'll have to study Mozart's scores and letters,
Memorize lines for all my leading men,

And learn to love those "pleasing lively dreams"
In which I slept... until I started to die.

In disbelief the men scrub their necks, chanting
"The Magic Flute" is a hymn to the occult,

To Catherine the Great and other cankerworms
Still infecting our imagination,

Still ravaging the forests the idle rich
Want to restore to their primeval state.

We won't be seduced again by celebrations
Of sorcery, perversion, and horsemanship.

Nor will we dance with the women in grass skirts
The arsonists imported from the Tropics,

Like mangoes and malaria. Don't worry:
We have our own torches for this affair—

Babushkas armed with battle-axes, black
Potatoes, faith; nuns focusing their burning

Glasses on fields of mown grass monks once named
Prayer; angels from the trenches in Ardennes;—

All of whom vow to take no prisoners
In the charade the count calls history:

The ball marking the anniversary
Of his descent into the catacombs,

Where in a pool of brilliant water sat
The alchemist's daughter, the heretic

Who showed him hermit's diaries, despots' wills,
Scripts of the past and future figured in

Cuneiform, which he could understand
Only until he left those galleries.

What he remembers is the candlelight
By which she turned his sermons into gold—

Our signal to escape from his estate,
Then form this picket line to stop his show.

And if that costs us our place in the coming
Revolt? Why should we care? Nothing will change:

Bright Glade will be a spa, while his woodlot
Furnishes coffins for the arsonists.

All we can do is rewrite our timetables
For the trains heading toward the afterlife,

And protest mining for uranium
In the rich veins of our religious texts...

Thus they return to picketing. The Cossack
Weeps for his horse. The diva clears her throat.

And in the courtyard cooks are sharpening
Their hatchets, talking of Michelangelo's—

Their favorite whorehouse in St. Petersburg.
A flock of headless chickens circles them.

The chef stuffs black bread in the mouths of crying
Maids he believes would rather steal his soul

Than peel another onion. *Resist not evil,*
He warns them. *The new world order is at hand!*

And it is: the ball opens with the report
Of rifles—and soldiers slumping to the ground.

Out of the traitors' pockets marbles roll.
The woodcutters collect them for the czar

And hide them in the samovar. The rising
Steam carries to the ceiling the cries of the dead.

That's where the diva looks for inspiration.
Hang from the chandelier Sicilian knives,

She tells the guests, Count Tolstoy's spirit fighters.
Not the gold effigy of Bonaparte!

But no one's listening. Music and mangoes
Are what they want, not pleas for insurrection.

So the Cossack, pocketing his silverware,
Winks at the diva, who begins a dirge

For the wolves starving in Siberia.
All the spirit fighters sing along.

———————

Midnight. The catacombs. The count in a fevered
Search for the alchemist's light or elixir,
His wife in buskins and a burlap shift,
Each careening on the drunken wing
Of history, reading the journals of the damned—

The soldiers bred for dancing and beheadings,
Not firing squads and impresarios
Disguised as anarchists from Madagascar,
Consumptive divas riding palominos,
A one-eyed coachman who claims to be the czar.

The count is tired of hearing from his fictions:
The serfs and toothless prostitutes he calls
His children; the censors, slaves, and penitents
Destined to battle for Byzantium;
The fat conductors of the afterlife;—
Why weren't those debts forgiven? he asks Sophia.
What made me fill my shelves with moneylenders,
Masks, and adulterers instead of saints?
Who were my sorcerer's apprentices?
Where did those women from the Tropics go?

She doesn't know. Or care. The Cossack, though,
Interests her more than any diarist.
Why did he shoot her windows out, she wonders,
Then steal her silverware and samovar?
Is he still hiding in these galleries?
Or has he fled to Rome and Istanbul?
And when the Sultan of Brunei announced,
Even the falling corpse of Russia will crush us!,
Why did the Cossack whinny at her maids,
And say he wished he had been Catherine's horse?

Meantime the diva coughing in the vault
Next door (*A harness and a heretic!*
The count declares), covered with blood and clutching
A bouquet of dried flowers from Bright Glade,
Prays that the picketers will rescue her
—And that she'll be remembered... What was the name
Of her adagio for striking miners,
Endangered beasts, and fire? *Air for the Thieves*
Of Calvary? Tone Poem with Cockatoo
And Wandering Jew? Resurrection Part II?

Forget the promises the alchemist
Made in the notes he left his only daughter,
The divinations no one understands—
The count and sad Sophia plan to transform
Their ball into a sermon on last things:
That stretch of dirty water our critics call
The future will become a slaughterhouse
For fish, imagination, and the new
World order in which saboteurs and lions
End up in the asylum! Sinners, repent!

The tropical women? Deep in *The Secret*
History of the Mongols, studying
Archery and the art of making war,
Imagining horse races on the steppe,
Shamans who can cure leprosy and coax
Spirits back from the dead, the bones of a wolf
Flayed on a monastery altar stone—
If only they could find the arsonists
Who vowed to burn the church and palace down!
Or board a train out of these catacombs!

They want to fly a biplane named *The Scourge*
Of God to Madagascar and beyond;
Drop leaflets in Red Square and Rome, describing
The serfs' emancipation, marriages
Between streetwalkers and noblemen, the setting
Of Tolstoy's next affair; trade in their axes
For tickets to the afterlife; then cry,
The dams are falling down in Istanbul
And Egypt, flooding saltworks, the bazaar,
And all the libraries in Babylon!

The water will drown horses, wolves, and pigs,
Slavers and slaves, the seamstresses in love
With spies sent by a minister in Minsk,
The carpenters and choreographers
Who built a fire out of the working plans

To stage a reading from the count's last book–
O who can lead us out of here by dawn?
And will we recognize you if our scars
Are gone? What shall we call you? Messiah? Isis?
O what soprano will sing for us now?

Will they escape before the Second Coming
Of Genghis Khan? Not if the one-eyed coachman,
Supervising the hasty burial
Of the czar's soldiers (and the firing squad
Poisoned by the mad chef and his spirit fighters),
Has any say about the catacombs.
He wants to keep them locked until Judgment Day.
No anchorite or Ishtar incarnation
Will make him change his mind. *Dig like gold miners!*
He tells the picketers. *Dig, traitors! Dig!*

The count and Genghis will have all the wild,
And time, and tombs in which to sleep or settle
Their nerves and debts, old scores, border disputes
Between the provinces of chance and China.
Theirs are the creeds, the empires of desire:
Persia means more to them than purgatory,
A cure for typhus, fire and brimstone scouring
Their names, their legends, from the Book of Hours,
The decadence of noblemen and nomads
Tired of the steppe, afraid of exploration...

They'll meet one afternoon at the train station
In Astapovo or the afterlife,
The count in buskins, cassock, and a cowl,
Genghis in silks and a sash made from the skins
Of sinners in Suez. Long-suffering
Sophia, dressed in black, will burn the leaflets
Leftover from the ball, while journalists
Question the despot, sage, and hermit summoned
From the vast desert of the past—disguised
As the czar, the one-eyed coachman, and the Cossack.

Truth... *I love much*—these were the count's last words,
And what he'll tell Genghis before they part
For hell and heaven, Borneo and Rome.
The Mongol conqueror will turn that phrase
Into a slogan for his next campaign
Across the steppe—for which he'll be the bard
If he can heave a discus far enough
To stop the train approaching from *The End*
And silence all the angels from Ardennes,
Who sing like wolves, like men: *Truth... I love much.*

The Author

Christopher Merrill's books include three collections of poetry, *Workbook, Fevers & Tides,* and *Watch Fire,* for which he received the Peter I. B. Lavan Younger Poets Award from the Academy of American Poets; translations of Aleš Debeljak's *Anxious Moments* and *The City and the Child;* several edited volumes, among them, *The Forgotten Language: Contemporary Poets and Nature;* and three books of nonfiction, *The Grass of Another Country: A Journey Through the World of Soccer, The Old Bridge: The Third Balkan War and the Age of the Refugee,* and *Only the Nails Remain: Scenes from the Balkan Wars.* He has held the William H. Jenks Chair in Contemporary Letters at the College of the Holy Cross, and now directs the International Writing Program at The University of Iowa. He and his wife, violinist Lisa Gowdy-Merrill, are the parents of two daughters, Hannah and Abigail.